HUMAN-MADE DISASTERS

INDUSTRIAL FIRES

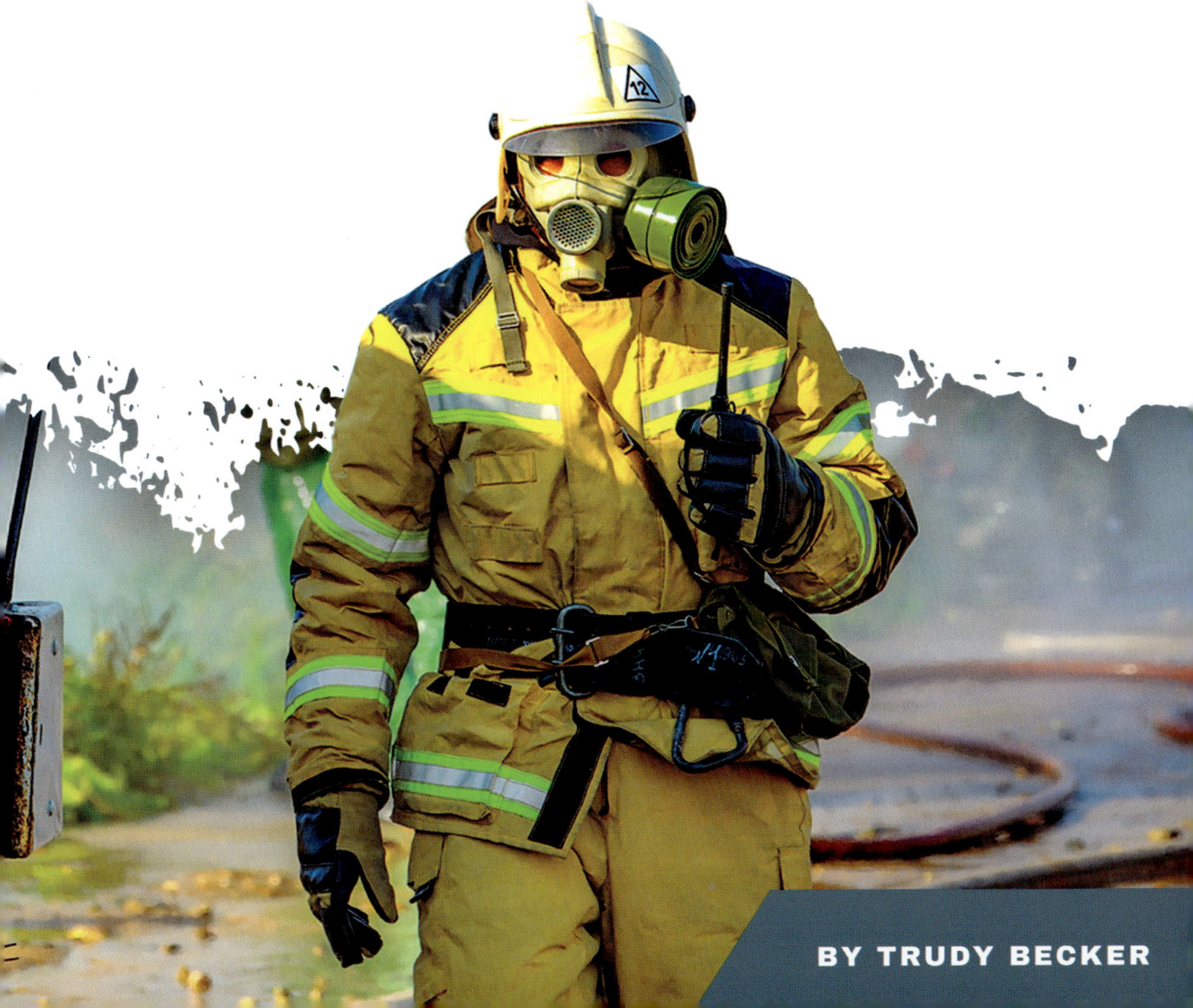

BY TRUDY BECKER

WWW.APEXEDITIONS.COM

Apex is distributed by North Star Editions:
sales@northstareditions.com | 888-417-0195

Produced for Apex by Red Line Editorial.

Photographs ©: Mauro Ujetto/NurPhoto/AP Images, cover; Shutterstock Images, 1, 8, 10–11, 12, 13, 14–15, 22–23, 24, 25, 26, 27; State Library of New South Wales, 4–5; Hulton Archive/Archive Photos/Getty Images, 6; RBM Vintage Images/Alamy, 9; AP Images, 16–17, 29; S. Mettler/Keystone/AP Images, 18–19; Hasan Raza/AP Images, 20–21

Library of Congress Control Number: 2023921776

ISBN
978-1-63738-925-6 (hardcover)
978-1-63738-965-2 (paperback)
979-8-89250-060-9 (ebook pdf)
979-8-89250-023-4 (hosted ebook)

Printed in the United States of America
Mankato, MN
082024

NOTE TO PARENTS AND EDUCATORS

Apex books are designed to build literacy skills in striving readers. Exciting, high-interest content attracts and holds readers' attention. The text is carefully leveled to allow students to achieve success quickly. Additional features, such as bolded glossary words for difficult terms, help build comprehension.

TABLE OF CONTENTS

CHAPTER 1

BLAZING FIRE

It is 1911. A group of young women cut fabric and sew clothes. They work for the Triangle **Shirtwaist** Company in New York City.

In the early 1900s, many workers sewed clothing by hand. They often worked in crowded spaces.

MEYERS
CROWN
&
WALLACH
HIGH STANDARD
CLOTHING
BLUM
CLOTHING
SPECIALTIES
23-29
HARRIS
BROS
MENS
CLOTHING
BERNSTEIN
& MEYERS
CLOAKS
SUITS
THE HATTERS' FUR EXCHANGE 23-29

Suddenly, the workers smell smoke. A scrap of fabric is burning. Fire spreads around the room. Huge flames rise up. Window glass shatters.

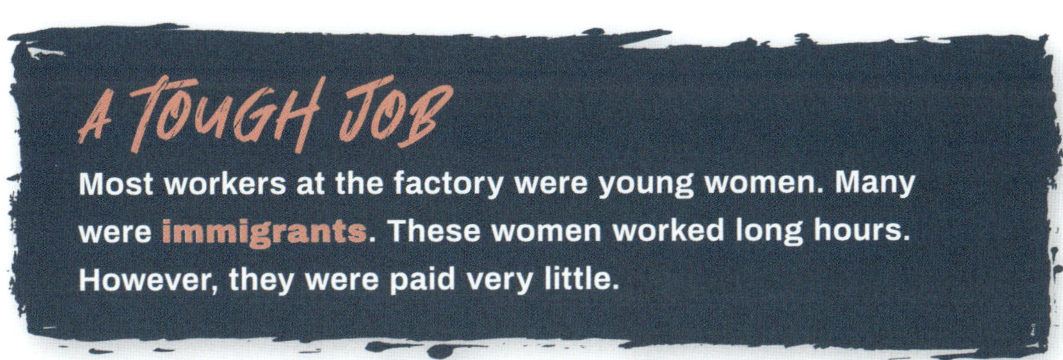

A TOUGH JOB

Most workers at the factory were young women. Many were **immigrants**. These women worked long hours. However, they were paid very little.

Firefighters rushed to the building. But their ladders could not reach the top floors.

Almost everything in the factory was destroyed.

The workers try to run. But some doors are locked. And the fire escape breaks. Many people are trapped as the fire blazes.

Many Americans were shocked by the fire. People called for stronger safety laws.

CHAPTER 2

HOW FIRES START

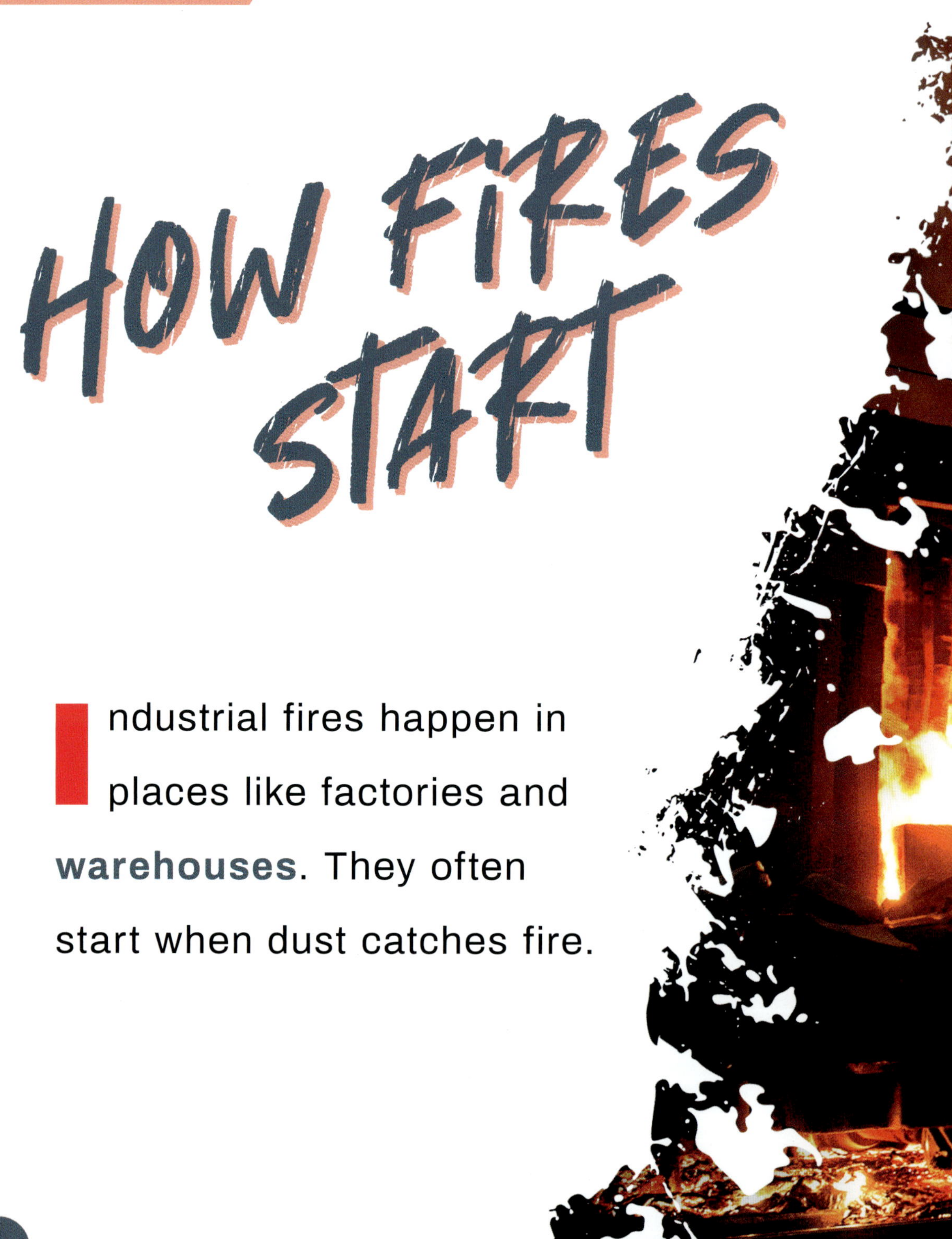

Industrial fires happen in places like factories and **warehouses**. They often start when dust catches fire.

Each year, industrial fires hurt hundreds of people in the United States.

Hot work can also cause fires. This work uses heat, flames, or sparks. Other causes include problems with electrical wires, outlets, or machines.

Welders use heat to connect pieces of metal together. Their tools send off sparks.

Machine parts moving against one another can create heat or sparks.

FAST FACT

Some factories use **flammable** chemicals. If they catch fire, they can explode.

Industrial fires can cause major damage. The fires kill or injure many people every year. They also harm the **environment**. They send out dangerous smoke and chemicals.

FAST FIRES

Factories that work with food or wood often create dust. This dust floats in the air. If it catches fire, the flames spread very quickly. Whole buildings can burn or explode.

Smoke from industrial fires can make people sick. People may have to leave nearby areas.

CHAPTER 3

PAST DISASTERS

In 1953, a fire burned a car factory in Livonia, Michigan. Welding sparks started it. The factory didn't have enough **firewalls**. Its whole roof collapsed.

The industrial fire in Livonia, Michigan, destroyed a car factory.

Another disaster happened in Switzerland in 1986. **Toxic** chemicals caught fire in a warehouse. Chemicals spread down a nearby river.

Chemicals from the fire in Switzerland washed into the Rhine River. They killed many fish and plants.

TOO WEAK

In 1977, a fire burned a car factory in Germany. The factory had many sprinklers. They began spraying right when the fire started. But the water streams were too weak to stop the flames.

The Dhaka fire began on the factory's ground floor. It spread up through nine stories.

In 2012, a huge fire blazed in Dhaka, Bangladesh. It scorched a clothing factory. The building did not have enough exits. More than 100 people died.

CHAPTER 4

A SAFER FUTURE

Firefighters arrive at industrial fires as soon as possible. But the fires can spread very rapidly. So, people work to **prevent** them.

Some companies have their own firefighters. They learn to deal with common causes of industrial fires.

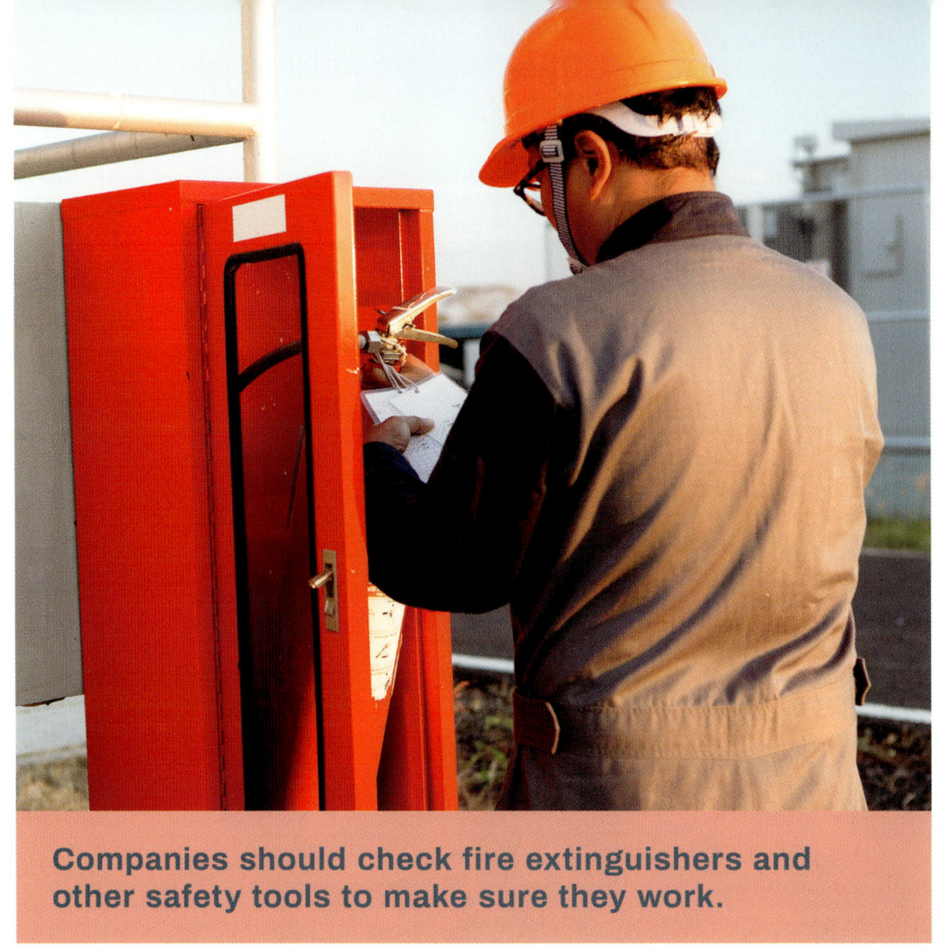

Companies should check fire extinguishers and other safety tools to make sure they work.

Cleaning up dust helps prevent fires. So does training workers. More training often leads to fewer mistakes. Factories can also stay safer by limiting hot work.

FAST FACT

Many factories do fire safety tests. They learn how quickly their machines could catch fire.

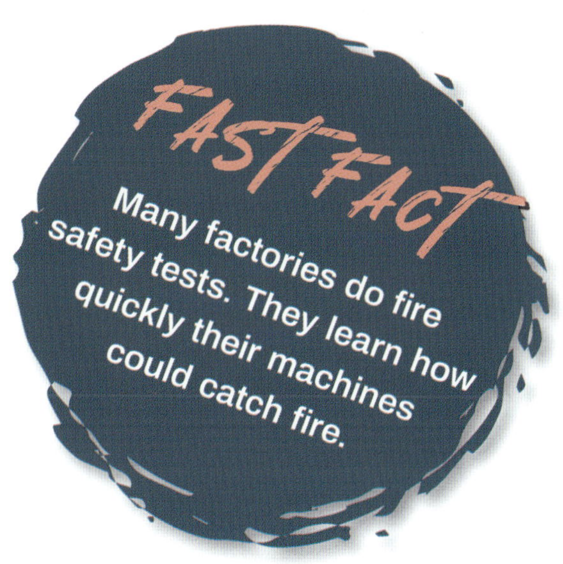

Some hot work uses melted rock or metal.

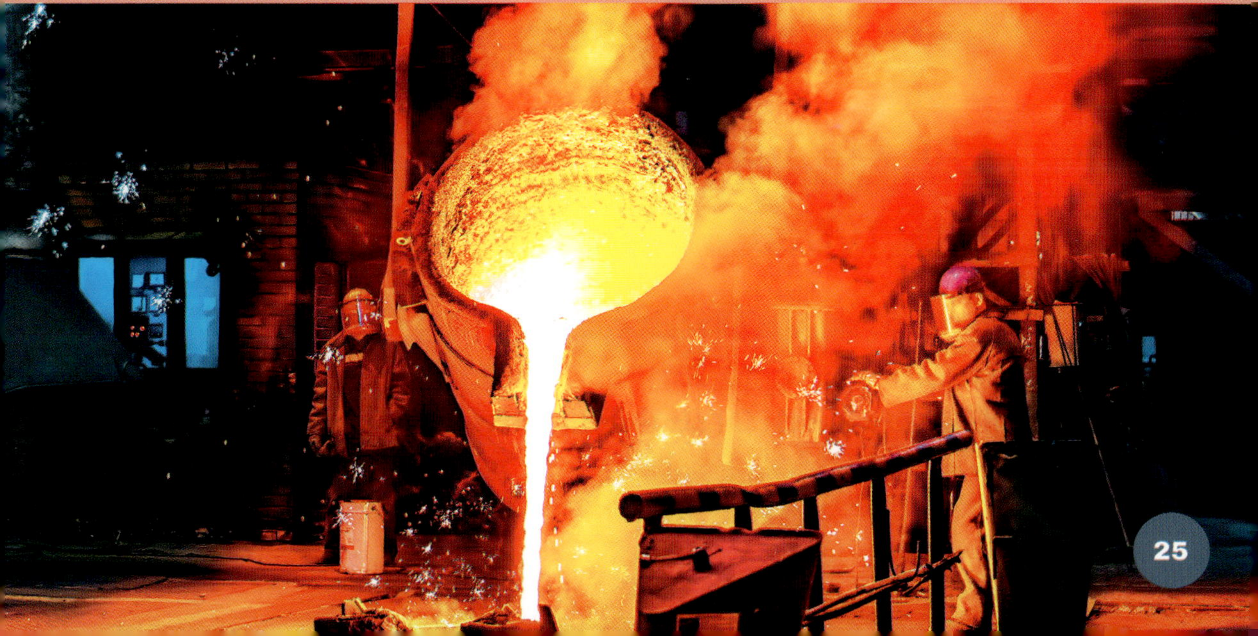

Many factories have automatic sprinklers. They spray water when they sense heat.

After some disasters, governments make new laws. For example, they might require new types of sprinklers or fire escapes. These changes help make factories safer.

CONTROLLING CHEMICALS

Burning chemicals can be dangerous. They can kill nearby plants and animals. So, laws limit the chemicals that companies can use and store. Companies must also avoid **polluting** nearby land and water.

Firefighters may wear masks to avoid breathing in harmful chemicals.

COMPREHENSION QUESTIONS

Write your answers on a separate piece of paper.

1. Write a few sentences explaining how industrial fires can start.

2. Which way of preventing fires do you think is the most important? Why?

3. When did the Triangle Shirtwaist Company's factory catch fire?

   A. 1911
   B. 1977
   C. 2012

4. How would limiting hot work make factories safer?

   A. There would be more factory workers.
   B. There would be fewer sparks that could spread.
   C. There would be less dust floating in the air.

5. What does **damage** mean in this book?

Industrial fires can cause major ***damage****. The fires kill or injure many people every year.*

- **A.** lots of money
- **B.** places to visit
- **C.** types of harm

6. What does **scorched** mean in this book?

In 2012, a huge fire blazed in Dhaka, Bangladesh. It ***scorched*** *a clothing factory.*

- **A.** helped
- **B.** burned
- **C.** moved

Answer key on page 32.

GLOSSARY

environment

The natural surroundings of living things.

firewalls

Walls that won't burn and can slow the spread of fires.

flammable

Able to catch fire easily.

immigrants

People who move to a new country.

polluting

Making dirty or unsafe.

prevent

To keep something from happening.

shirtwaist

A type of old-fashioned shirt with buttons.

toxic

Harmful or poisonous.

warehouses

Large buildings where people or companies store things.

BOOKS

Lewis, Mark L. *Fire Rescues*. Mendota Heights, MN: Focus Readers, 2020.

Murray, Julie. *Great Chicago Fire.* Minneapolis: Abdo Publishing, 2024.

Pettiford, Rebecca. *Wildfires*. Minneapolis: Bellwether Media, 2020.

ONLINE RESOURCES

Visit **www.apexeditions.com** to find links and resources related to this title.

ABOUT THE AUTHOR

Trudy Becker lives in Minneapolis, Minnesota. She likes exploring new places and loves anything involving books.

INDEX

ANSWER KEY:
1. Answers will vary; 2. Answers will vary; 3. A; 4. B; 5. C; 6. B